WHITE SHADOWS, BLACK SHADOWS

Translations

THE DARK CHILD (Camara Laye)
THE RADIANCE OF THE KING (Camara Laye)
A DREAM OF AFRICA (Camara Laye)
MEMOIRS OF A DUTIFUL DAUGHTER (Simone de Beauvoir)
THE HEAVENLY MANDATE (Erwin Wickert)
THE TALES OF HOFFMAN
THE LITTLE MAN (Erich Kästner)
DAILY LIFE OF THE ETRUSCANS (Jacques Heurgon)
DAILY LIFE IN THE FRENCH REVOLUTION (Jean Robiquet)
MICHAEL KOHLHAAS (Kleist)
SELECTED WRITINGS OF JULES SUPERVIELLE

WHITE SHADOWS,

露木茂

BLACK SHADOWS

Poems of Peace and War

JAMES KIRKUP

LONDON: J. M. DENT & SONS LTD

First published in 1970
© James Kirkup, 1970

Made in Great Britain
at the
Aldine Press · Letchworth · Herts
for
J. M. DENT & SONS LTD
Aldine House · Bedford Street · London

SBN: 460 03914 8

Acts 8. On the Baptized Ethiopian

Let it no longer be a forlorn hope
                To wash an Ethiop:
He's washt. His gloomy skin a peaceful shade
                For his white soul is made:
And now, I doubt not, the Eternal Dove,
                A black-fac'd house will love.

Richard Crashaw: *Divine Epigrams*

The Little Black Boy

My mother bore me in the southern wild,
And I am black, but O! my soul is white;
White as an angel is the English child,
But I am black, as if bereav'd of light . . .

I'll shade him from the heat, till he can bear
To lean in joy upon our Father's knee;
And then I'll stand and stroke his silver hair,
And be like him, and he will then love me.

William Blake: *Songs of Innocence*

In Memory of
Two Joes
Ackerley and Orton

ACKNOWLEDGMENTS

'White Shadows' appeared in *The Poetry Review, Poetry Australia, Workings* and *Peace News*.

'Frogs in Thailand Commit Mass Suicide' and 'Young Lovers' Fiery Death Protest Against War' appeared in *Expression*.

'Short Story', 'Damn the Culture Ministry' and 'The Core of the Matter' appeared in *Poetry Nippon*.

'Windows in Manhattan' appeared in *Mundus Artium*.

'Baby's Drinking Song' appeared in *The Listener*.

'A Windowcleaner in Wall Street' appeared in *The New York Times*.

'Death's Little Irony' appeared in *Workings*.

'Christ Rejected' and 'Lonely Boy' appeared in *Poetry Singapore*.

'The Beautiful Strangers' appeared in *Cosmic Brotherhood International* (Yokohama) and in *Frontier of Going, An Anthology of Space Poetry* (Panther Books).

'In the House of Emily Dickenson', 'Elegy for Emily' and 'At the Grave of Emily Dickenson' appeared in *Workings* and *Poetry Australia*.

CONTENTS

LEGENDS

CONTRADICTIONS

SIGNS OF DEATH

CHE LIVES!

A deposition. But
No virgin's arms
To hold him, raise him up.

No mother's tears to fall
Upon the white napkin,
Linen-folded, hanging
From her lustrous eye,
Lips bleached in agony.

All here is formal, factual.
No grief.
No sorrowing followers
Wrap his corpse.

Not nobly naked.
The young body
Still crumples its stained
Uniform at armpit and crotch.

No friend to care.
No love to weep.

An exasperated official
Nipping offended nostrils
With slim white fingers:
Gesture of blowing
Rich snot from a bad nose.

Hand holding nose:
Primitive master tells us,
In his modern medieval way,
Yes, death stinks.

In an obscure corner
The centurion pisses,
His horse with raised tail
Drops dumplings of dung.

3

At the martyr's head,
Reporters, secret agents.
A magazine photographer
Kneels by his side,
But not in prayer—
Only to record
Illumination's
Fleshlit immobility.

Finer and graver than them all,
Wearing a secret smile.
That man whose open eyes
Look not, but see.
That visionary face, white
In the curling frame of
Black hair, black beard.

The dead are dead.
But that does not matter.
The dead do not speak,
But that too
Does not matter.

What matters
Is that he lived and spoke
And walked among us on this earth.

At the resurrection
No one will mistake him
For a gardener.

Behold the man.
Even in death
Che lives.

WANDERERS: IN MEMORIAM, ROBERT F. KENNEDY

Sirhan Sirhan, your name in Arabic means a wanderer.
Why did you have to have the face of a poet,
The head of an unavenging angel?

A face white as death, head of black curls, eyes
White as fear, black as time—negative of that other face,
Of the head, the eyes of the man you killed.

You, a thin, poor youth, a wandering stranger of twenty-four.
He, a famous middle-aged man, millionaire of distinguished
    family.
Neither of you particularly good or bad, handsome or clever.

Just average humans. Both decent men in your different ways.
Your father was surprised to remember you were always a good
    boy.
Yes. Your face is not the face of a killer: an ordinary stranger's.

His face was always the face of the victim. The eyes were
    doomed,
Like those of his murdered brother, whose familiar face
Looked through that friendly mask, the open smile.

Shadows both, born to wander towards each other, to meet
At that common moment, in a crowded hotel pantry. Of all
Places. A meeting that was your first, his last.

Parting is the beginning of meeting.
Meeting is the beginning of parting.
Wanderings end in strangers meeting.

*

His wounded head, bleeding on the pantry floor,
Had a new nobility it never showed in life, in which
We viewed him always as the good all-American guy.

5

Your hunted face, wide-eyed, open-mouthed,
Framed in the strongarm suits of his supporters' arms,
Had another kind of dignity: one man against the world.

The world is with you now. The world is too much with you
    now.
Those who are most against you are those most with you.
No. You can never be a wanderer again.

*

Why did you do it? Why was it he who had to die?
It was not you who did it. It was not he who had to die.
It was another hand that held the gun, another blood that fell.

It was the wandering blood of bombs and bullets.
It was the wandering poisons, rockets, bacteria, napalm.
It was the wandering soldier slaughtering his brother.

It was the million hands that hold the guns of war.
It was the million violences that destroy each day.
It was the million innocents who fall each hour.

The children of earth play dangerous games.
The children of earth have killing toys.
There is no place, no peace, no rest

For wanderers of death in games of war.

WHITE SHADOWS

*On a photograph of the white shadow left by a
man annihilated by the atom bomb in Hiroshima*

*

It was another morning, another morning.
A morning like any other, of dust and death.
A morning of war: raids, speeches, warnings.
In wartime, all mornings are alike.

You were crossing a bridge in Hiroshima,
A bridge of plain cement, a place without mystery.
Below, the grey river ran as always, going somewhere,
Metalled and moved by the early summer sun.

The sun, that cast your shadow clearly, a healthy black.
It was the shadow of a complete man, someone
With a life, a personality, a past: but
Moving through a present that could have no future.

What were you thinking? Were you feared, hated, loved?
Were you late for work? Sad or sick? Artist, student?
Photographer or newsman returning home after a night out?
What was your plan for the day? Who were you, shadow?

I do not know your name, your age, your blood type.
And now I shall never see your face, hear your voice.
No one will ever know your name, your age, your blood type.
And are there any left who remember your face, your voice?

Now, the name, the face, the voice no longer matter.
A 'plane drilled the blue, as they often did. The river ran.
Your shadow was black: then white—the flash was all
And nothing. You were not there to hear the rest.

Your shade—poor, forked human creature—fled
Like a mist of dew on morning glories. Your breath
Evaporated, taken away, lost soul, before
You even had time to scream. Your shade was white.

*

That white
Is blacker than black,
That shadow
Is more than a shade.

That shape
Is whiter than white.
That whiteness
Is blacker than night.

Blacker than black,
Blacker than white.
Blacker than blast and blight,
Blacker than light.

Whiter than black,
Whiter than sight,
Black as the flash,
Blacker than fright.

White as the bomb,
White as a scar,
Black as the womb,
Black as war.

Blacker than breath,
Blacker than cold.
Whiter than death,
Whiter than gold.

That white
Is blacker than black,
That shadow
Is more than a shade.

*

You vanished, and a whole world, a fragrance, a name
Vanished with you. A shade. It was death indeed,
Death in absence.—But you left behind you, in the black rain
Of ash, your own memorial, your own white shadow.

It stretched companionless across the road, until
Its head (hatless) was lost over the edge of the bridge.
Yours was the long shadow of early morning, another morning,
Another morning in early summer, when shadows are blackest.

The white shadow shows no feet. You were already a ghost.
(In Japan, they say, ghosts have no feet.)—No arms.
Only the elementary fork, the primitive crotch,
And the torso, naked, alone, archaic. No hero's.

*

Who owns him? Was he your father? Your brother?
Your lover, was he? Your enemy, friend, classmate?
Was this white memory once your husband of flesh and blood?
All I know is, he was a man, a human being like myself.

Questions are hard, but it is worse to remain silent.
Nor can we afford not to look. We must see all, and say all
To satisfy the dead who died with such indignity, the shades
That are watching us, white and speechless. We cannot look away.

*

You whose shadow once was black as soot,
Black the vivid black of all living shadows—
You whose shadow moved beside you everywhere
Like a favourite hound at heel, mysterious, silent.

You exchanged your shadow and your shape,
O Peter Schlemihl, for one no longer black,
For the white shadow that is waiting here
In all of us today, in all of us today.

We too have sold our shadows to the devil.
We have gained the whole world
But lost the fragrance of our immortal souls.
A race without shadows, we too are doomed.

Led by the ignorant and mad, we live in worlds
Where black is white, and white is black,
Where leaders say that peace can not be found
Except in continued bombings of the helpless.

Where war is peace, and peace is war,
Where bombs are good, and people bad.
Where sleep is wake and eat is starve.
Where live is die. Where love is kill.

*

We look upon this calm, white monument
And see in it an image of ourselves.
Today, our shadows walk beside us still,
But they are no longer black, no longer black.

We are all white shadows, anonymous as yours.
No longer human, we cross bridges, walk in our shadows' snow.
Grey rivers are metalled and moved by the sun. It is
Another morning. And all our mornings are alike.

Tokyo
December 6, 1967

YOUNG LOVERS' FIERY DEATH PROTEST
AGAINST WAR

With all their clothes on—
Unusual for these two, so frank in passion and
Most eloquent when naked—they put their arms
Round one another, lay down among the derelicts
Of a used-car dump. Silently. Japan jumped all about them.
It was the neon midnight of New Year's Eve.

The temple bells, banged by severe monks,
Slowly massaged the icy air
With warm waves of vibrations,
A steady storm of breakers on Pacific shores.

One hundred and eight notes,
To the number of one year's sins:
How small a number for one man, how small!
They welled like giant teardrops, one
Upon the other, sounding a wilderness of nothing.
Stars creaked like hard snow underfoot.

The squashed cars cast shadows of traffic accidents,
A nightmare of horns forever silenced, brakes rusted,
Lights dipped once and for all, internal combustion
Finally busted, big ends gone, tyres flat
As rats ironed out on city expressways,
Windscreens riddled, galaxied, steering columns
Snapped. No rearview mirrors. Modern Japan.

He had placed beside them a can of gasoline
Whose tremulous tin occasionally clanged
Cold notes of unearthly plangency, wailings
That mingled with the welling bells
Or sang like firecrackers, pistol shots.

In the can a pale green plastic siphon was
Already inserted, leaning like a flower in a vase.
As the bells tolled, the liquid rose, and pulsed
Like icy piss over their winter rags.

On that one hundred and eighth stroke, or just before,
She raised a hand blue with cold and neon,
And, with a gesture too benumbed to be like
Defiant snapping of her fingers, clicked and sparked
The cheap lighter in the form of a jewelled pistol.

Asakusa

FROGS IN THAILAND COMMIT MASS SUICIDE

(Newspaper report)

to Kusano Shinpei

How wise they are!
Knowing the end is near
They exterminate themselves, rather
Than face the ignominy of atomic death.

These frogs once lived a happy life.
They ate, drank, bred and croaked in freedom,
They hadn't a care in the world.
They were always great jumpers.
That is why
They had such long,
Noble, meaty thighs.
How they loved to jump!

But in their blissful existence
Came a cloud, a sadness, a sick fear
Of an uncertain but terrible future.

They were helpless.
There was nothing they could do
To save themselves, except
To jump, and jump and jump.

They used their springs of flesh
To hurl themselves upon the piercing,
Foot-long spines of
One thorny bush.

Such a bush in the tropics
Has thousands of fierce spikes.
But there were not enough to accommodate
The frogs' mad rush of despair.

So they played a macabre leapfrog,
Thrusting themselves upon each other,
Death-coitus on spits of thorn,
Until there were scores of frogs,
Pitiful Saint Sebastians, arrow-pierced,
On every long spine's lancing dirk.

It was a poignant *auto-da-fé*.
As if on long darts or vicious needles
They were impaled through the heart,
Skewered for some atomic barbecue.

Like rats abandoning a sinking ship,
Like lemmings drowning in Norwegian fjords.
—Had the impending visit of the God of War,
President Lyndon B. Johnson of the United States of America,
Put the fear of hell into the innocents?
For it was another Massacre of the Innocents,
Another St Bartholomew's Eve!

*

Only the week before,
So the informed sources say,
Frogs and toads by their tens of thousands
Fought losing battles with each other,
Great armies of frogs and toads
Fighting insensately, killing each other off
In a war to end all frog wars.
No one was spared
In these losing battles with despair,
Battles fought to the death.

What could they see
That we poor mortals cannot see?
What have they heard? Some whisper of fright,
Some ghastly rumour we shut our ears to?
What have they tasted on the air—
A tang of radioactive dust?
Have they seen white shadows,
Shades of black ash,
Ghosts of atomic rain?

13

Why cannot we see
What they have seen,
And stop before it is too late?
Are we helpless as frogs?
Why cannot we hear what they have heard?
Is it a sound beyond human hearing,
That only frogs can catch?
Why cannot we taste
The contaminated air of hydrogen bomb holocausts?
Are we, too,
With all our wealth of wars and want,
Helpless as gentle frogs and peaceable toads?

*

May our leaders take a lesson
From this augury and omen, and
From these creatures' brave example.
There have been stern critics
Of the moral rectitude of such mass assassinations,
Who say such things are permissible
Only when hydrogen bombs are dropped.
But I say it was not suicide.
They were right to prefer death to
Deadly life or living hell,
To be true ghosts,
Not white shadows in blackened sepulchres.
Better to kill oneself than to exist
Pitifully in fear and misery and pain,
Than to be slaughtered en masse,
Inhumanly, insanely, by
A manicured finger on a plastic button.

We are all frogs and toads.
We mean no harm to anyone, but we are all
Impaled, transfixed already
Upon the thorns of death, the pale
Spires of unbelief. Like Shelley,
We fall upon the thorns of life, we bleed . . .

Bleed to death upon the thorns
That we alone have grown
In this former garden of our pleasant earth.

Boxing Day, 1967

LONELY BOY, 12, COMMITS SUICIDE

(Japanese newspaper report)

Deepwinter snows
In dark Hokkaido.

At the primary school
You learned to read and write.

Lamplit classroom, warm stove.
Deep country in the darks of snow.

'I am lonely.' That is all
You could tell your classmates.

They could do nothing.
They were lonely too.

But you did something about it.
You learned your last lesson.

You had loneliness by heart.
. No one knew it better than you.

In the dark barn in Ohno Town,
Alone for ever, you hanged yourself.

Deepwinter snows
In dark Hokkaido.

DEATH OF A LONG-DISTANCE RUNNER

*in memory of Tsuburaya Kokichi,
placed third in the Tokyo Olympics
marathon, who died by his own hand*

Life is short
And art is long.

Life's track is the longest
Distance between two points.

To break death's tape
We have to run the strongest race.

From the starter's pistol
To the instant when all snaps

Is only a step.
A long journey is its first step.

As the arrow from the bow
Is always at rest, always

To run well is to stay at rest.
—Now you are at rest.

Death is greater than the Ethiop victor,
Or fair-haired fate, the British overreacher.

You have run your race.
But still you are running well.

Breast the tape for the last time.
The applause is silence.

Life is short
And art is long.

BLACK SHADOWS

in memory of Martin Luther King

I can hear from New Orleans
Funeral jazz.

Memphis, Nashville, Atlanta
Blow horns of grief.

All the jazzbands of the South
Trumpet your murder.

What has our world become? Are we all mad?
Good man, forgive us.

*

When I look at your calm face, I see
The courage of your death.

It is our shame
That such courage was necessary.

You knew that bullet from a white rifle
Would one day seek your flesh.

You walked in danger every day
With sad humility.

Not wishing to be chosen thus by fate,
Yet knowing you must drink that cup.

Your wife and children weep now
For a man who was more than a father.

You were a father to all of us.
We did not know it till you were gone.

Now we understand your gentleness
Too late. Why must we hate?

17

Why must we kill our brothers?
Why suffer this shame of wars upon wars?

*

You who told us war and violence are bad
Died of war and violence.

You were a man of peace and mercy,
But received neither.

Let us raise no monument to you
But human peace and mercy.

What has our world become? Are we all mad?
Good man, forgive us.

THE CORE OF THE MATTER

'A Pregnant Black Was Heart Donor. Recipient in
Capetown A White Ex-policeman.' (*New York Times headline*)

The sources said
Black mother with child
Delivered of her heart.

Informed hospital sources said
She had died earlier in the day.
A haemorrhage of the brain.

How did the heart survive?
What cupped its blood?
The sources do not say.

Telltale heart translated
Into the ribcage of a white
Ex-policeman, age fifty-two.

She lost her heart
But not to him to whom
She lost her heart.

We know his name, his family,
His address. Not hers.
'Sources said they did not know
Whether her family had been traced.'

All we know now is
She was black,
About thirty-two years old,
Thirty-two weeks gone.

The sources also said
They did not know
What happened to the unborn child.

A child ripped untimely
From his mother's heart.

Sources said the donor's
'Advanced state of pregnancy
Made her a suitable
Type of donor because blood
Circulation is best in pregnancy.'

Blood from a pregnant woman
Is the best juice available,
Black or white.
Black will do as well as white.
In the dark of death
All hearts are alike,
All blood is red.

All hearts are red.
The hearts of pregnant women
Are full to overflowing.

In the right place, her heart
'Started beating spontaneously
And normally,' so the sources said.

Proud to be white,
No longer anonymous?
Not mother-passioned now,
But fathered-forth?

'Hearts are not had as a gift . . .'
But hers was.
Unsolicited.

To segregate, the sources say, is 'to
Separate from the general body'.
Certainly she
Was segregated.
So was her heart.

Miscegenation of the heart
Is just exchange,
'One for the other giv'n . . .'

But segregation
Here was integration.
'There never was a better bargain driv'n.'

—Can we take heart from this,
Learn a lesson it never tried to teach,
That black is white
And white is black

And one day
The twain shall meet?

What do the sources say?

DEATH'S LITTLE IRONY

In Memoriam: Thomas Hardy

Laid away in Poets' Corner,
His body, as it had been willed,
Was to be the nation's.
But his heart, cut out for death,
Was to be buried with his love's
Bare bones in a Wessex grave.
    In a florid meat-dish, there it lay
    On the kitchen table, vexed no more.

It lay there alone, unbeating,
In the empty house, watched only
By his grim ghost, helpless as a babe.
—When parson and sexton came
To take the heart for burial,
They found it gone, and the cat
    Licking his chops . . . So
    They buried the cat.

SIGNS OF LIFE

DAMN THE CULTURE MINISTRY

My lover from Asakusa, a blooming boy,
He who adorned his amber body
With a swirling tattoo
Of the goddess Kwannon surrounded
By ferns, wildflowers, flags,
And had a capering carp
Illuminating each vigorous buttock—

He whose suit of ink,
Blue and black and dogrose pink,
Was the one garment
I could not divest him of—
When he pulled back
His periwinkled foreskin, he discovered,
Always with a broken smile,
A gay butterfly on the *glans penis*.

Now the Culture Ministry
Has proclaimed him
Not only a National Treasure, but
An Intangible National Treasure!

Now I can no longer
Hold him in my arms like a warm
Sheaf of poppies and wheat, no more
Stroke that golden-amber shoulder
Stained with a lace of sugarbag blue,
No more bedew
With tears and kisses his
Empurpled butterfly . . .

I can't get my hands on him.
Our love is finished,
Broken by banal politicians.

Now he belongs to the Nation,
Which means he belongs to no one,
And especially not to me.

I always put him on a pedestal,
But not like this!
He might as well be behind glass,
Stuffed and docketed in the National Museum.

Damn the Culture Ministry!

HOTWATER HEAVEN

We got into the big wooden tub together.
It was full of very hot water, and so
We could hardly help making love.

What started off
As a drunken joke
Became sober truth.
A delightful extra
We hadn't expected—
At least I hadn't.

Though big, the tub
Was small for two.
Fortunately, we both
Have boyish bodies.

Her pink nipples
Nibbled the surface of
The wood-scented water hoary with steam
Like the grasping mouths of hungry carp
And her black hair
Floated every-which-way,
Beside itself with bliss.

I was only afraid we'd burst the bath.
But the wooden staves
Were carpentered to last for ever.

There was no language barrier,
For there was no need for words.

Afterwards, I wondered if it was forbidden
To copulate in a Japanese bathtub.
Coition is somehow so surgical.

When we got out, there was almost no water left in the bathtub.
We'd squeezed and splashed it all out in our fish-like tangles,
Salmon, carp
Repeatedly leaping the falls in springtime.

So we filled it with fresh.

I'm sure the god of the bathroom didn't mind,
Because he allowed us to be so happy.

ROBATA REVISITED

for Tomiya Amae

As I enter your house once more,
After years of absence,
The thick rope curtain
Whips my shoulders and bowed head.

You, the master of the mysteries
Of food and drink and all creation,
Are still sitting there, where I left you,
Beside the fire, like a god of the hearth.

On the rush-matted floor, you are surrounded,
Still, by your big grey flagons of rice-wine.
You extend the wooden ladle with the long handle:
Your only handshake, distant, yet strong.

*

Master, you have not changed.
You are still dressed in suits of invisibility.
Yet you are visible indeed: your cropped head like a boy's.
You have the dignity of everlasting youth.

Nor has your house changed. The grave, gay,
Human symbols of fertility preside like deities.
Your customers still sit around your platform
As if at a play in which you are the only star.

Here in this legendary, magic place
We are most at ease when on our best behaviour.
The light is dim, the paper doors are dark,
But your laughter is, as always, bright.

*

All who enter here
Become part of a secret.
All who bow and enter here, as
At a shrine, participate in ancient mysteries.

28

If you will allow me to return,
I shall not stay away so long next time.
In my absence I have often thought of you,
Reigning like a merman in your cavern of creation.

On your long ladle, extended like a god's hand,
I have put my heart in payment;
And received in return, without asking for anything,
The priceless gift of your awareness.

Sendai, June 1967

SHORT STORY

I walked past the house where,
It is said,
A boy was inventively murdered
By his young manlover.

His body was found
On the *tokonoma*
Chopped up into eight hundred and eighty pieces.

His balls
And his still-trembling prick
Were artfully arranged
On the spikes of a flower-holder,
A flower arrangement
In the style of the Sogetsu school,
Decorated only
With stains ripped from
His old pair of rayon bikini pants.

Beside all this,
A candle stood, lighted,
And jasmine incense was burning,
And the *kakemono*
Was of the conventional kind,
Such as may be bought anywhere
On the streets of Asakusa—
A leaping carp.

Now, it is said,
An ordinary Japanese family
Lives contentedly in that house.

The housing situation is so difficult,
One cannot very well pick and choose.

The husband is a salaried employee
Of a middling-great company manufacturing
Something to do with plastic lavatory deodorants.

She, once weekly, attends
Classes in flower arrangement
In the style of the Sogetsu school.
And they have two perfect children, both girls,
Who do their homework diligently, zealously,
Night after night after night.

The house is always clean as a new pin.
The *tokonoma* always dusted,
Arranged with a *kakemono* of a leaping carp.
Such as may be bought on any street in Asakusa,
And decorated with seasonal flowers—
Plum, cherry, iris, chrysanthemum—mingled
With bits of old wood, barbed wire, rusty nails,
Cement blocks, old bicycle tyres.
Sections of cantilever bridges,
Mobiles of fluorescent plastic.

Beside such elaborate arrangements
The telephone, coiled like a cat;
The portable TV set flickers
Like a pale-blue hydrangea in a pot:
Batman, monsters, happy household equipment,
Insane commercials.

This is a fairly typical
Japanese family scene.

TO MY CHILDREN UNKNOWN, PRODUCED BY ARTIFICIAL INSEMINATION

To my children unknown:
Space projects,
My galactic explosions—
I do not even know
How many of you there are,
If ever you got off the launching pad.

All I know is,
As a 'donor'
I received acknowledgement of
'The success of the experiment'.
All boys.
Mission completed.

I gave my all.
Under rigid scientific conditions,
In the interests of science I
Was willingly raped:
The exciting suction pump
In a stark laboratory,
Sterile,
Beneath blazing lights,
Masked assistants all eyes.

That laboratory bench
Was the only home I ever made,
My single marriage bed.

A kind of actor, I performed,
Projected my part.
All systems were go.
And come. My role,
The onlie begetter
Of these ensuing
Moppets.

All happiness! Yes—
After the initial mild embarrassment
At making an exhibition of myself
(In front of all those students!)
Despite the public nature of the occasion
And the scientific dispassion
I endured with moody willingness
The blastoff of private pleasure
That sent me to the point of no return
And even beyond,
Back to where I came from,
Into outer space.

My sample deepfrozen, docketed
Even before the almost endless countdown
Of detumescence.
I was advised, clinically speaking,
Not to think of 'her'
As 'the wife', but only as
'The recipient'. The tool
Simply as 'the reproductive mechanism',
My essential juices
'Prime sperm' (Caucasian).

On to the Womb, the Moon!
Countdown to zero! Takeoff!
Rockets away! Man in space!
Into orbit! Gee, what a view!
Back to the Womb, the Moon!
To the Lake of Sleep,
The Marsh of Death,
The Sea of Showers.
The trip one long ejaculation . . .

*

Why do I never wonder who you are, wives—
You whose great bowl of a thousand wombs
Bled to a stitch in time?
Even before the nuptial night

33

Our divorce was final. Could I care much less
About the offspring of my loins, sprigs
Of a poet's side-job? I feel your absence
Only as I might feel amputated limbs.

At least I'm spared
The patter of tiny feet.

*

Get lost,
Scions of my poetry, my poverty.
I was well paid to engender you.
(Non-taxable income from personal assets.)

Better for us never
To know a father. If only
You could never know your mother!

So be nice, be clever.
Adventurers, in setting forth
Have never a thought for your begetter.
But zoom on in that eternity
Promised by your patron, your donor,
By your ever-dying poet
Who remains
Your humble servant.

BABY'S DRINKING SONG

for a baby learning for the first time to drink
from a cup

(*Vivace*)

Sip a little
Sup a little
From your little
Cup a little
Sup a little
Sip a little
Put it to your
Lip a little
Tip a little
Tap a little
Not into your
Lap or it'll
Drip a little
Drop a little
On the table
Top a little.

AMERICA AMERICA

THE AMATEUR PHOTOGRAPHER

Stalk the light and
Waylay shifting glooms.
Images, angles, shots.
Mainstreets, haunted rooms.

Crouch, kneel, crane.
Filter the fabulous hues
For the colorpic lobelias,
Geraniums in the public eye,
Misty lad's-love, aromatic
Dews of sops-in-wine.
Sunflowers gyrating as
Time makes them click.

Pot the Capitol, a snip, and
Take the Pentagon.
On your belly, with bread,
Con the squirrels in the Park.
Shutter the famous poet
Fullface on office balcony,
Wide sun in his smile, a
Wind from the west in his tie.

The camerafiend thieves,
Stores in the darkroom
Moonback of his mind
Trick tumbles, handheld slips,
Running close-ups, stills
Of women catnapping, dead
Natures with a twist—that Benjamin
Franklin in stained marble breeches.

Till the Great Lensman
Has shot his load, his
Ruck and reel of endless
Patterns and plights, culled

In a spool, a pool
Of undeveloped night's
Half-frame interludes,
The slides of sight.

Rewinding his expense
Of vision finds a waste
Of time. (Having forgotten
To put a film in.)

APPARITIONS

The summer was only a block away.
There was a sun, somewhere, but—
Round about the middle reaches
Of skyscrapers, tops lost in gardens,
Clouds swam in their own rain.

A fun fog
Glazed the windows
With a billion gazers' breaths,
While out of gratings at
Crux of avenue and street
Huffed underground volcanoes.

Yellowcabs pounced through steam like
Clowns through damp paper hoops,
Leaving curled wisps trailing,
Failing, melting along the wet block,
Vamping the street signs
With the wildwool locks of smoke
On a witch's pan of boiling rainwater.

*

Through the fog, steam and rain,
With a pocket of strange coins and weightless tokens
I mooned my first
Metropolitan day, my shade
Accosted frequently by shades,
People wanting to know things,
Asking me how to get
To where I had no thought of going.

Sometimes, to conceal my strangeness
And ignorance, I just informed them
It was only a block away,
And they were surprised
To find it was so near.
I was surprised too.

*

Those graves of sights, the avenues,
The cement clouds crammed
With sparks of light and the silent
Thunder of elevators.

The cool electric news
Like a streaming headcold
Washing its mustardbath reflections
Between my soaked shoes:
That's life, that was.

Blasts from airconditioned banks
Sneezed on my fevers.
With packaged liquors,
Loans, and sandwiches to go,
A skyline of broken teeth
Combed the hard birds
Out of the mad hair of heroes.
In minor parks,
Statues with hats on
Drowned in village trees.

Distances were great.
A white tower vast as the sky
Seemed only a block away.
Yet to reach it took
One livelong day.

*

I ate poundcake in the automat.
It still lingers in my mouth
With a taste of money.

*

Was I human? I felt
Like someone from another planet.
Though I could speak the language,
For days I never spoke.
I was always only a block away.

Yet a stranger in a plastic showerbonnet
Called me honey, as if
It was the normal thing,
Asking me the way
To the Cathedral of St John the Divine.
I must have looked as if I belonged.
To a lost person,
Everyone else belongs,
No one else is alone.

I was gazing at the greenparks
Through the shut face of
Museum windows crying in the rain.
I was watching someone
Out in the birdbath park,
Someone running urgently
With rolled-up sleeves,
Looking behind him from time to time
Guiltily, as if from the scene of a crime,
A black man
Pursued by his own shadow, both beautiful.

But then, far away, small as a star,
He stopped to do pushups.
He will do pushups till kingdom come.

*

You ok honey?
When I tried to answer her—I knew well
The Cathedral of St John the Divine—
My hands flapping like fish
In the mesh of the tourist map,
My voice was more than a block away,
And always too low.
Pardon me, honey, you British?

*

I cannot rise above
This hive of loneliness.
I see behind me dark people
With dark faces out of a dark past,
Shadows reflected with my own
In the sleeping pool
Of a famous picture glazed
With time's reproductions.

I turn towards them, and her,
But they look at me as if
I am the great Picasso nude
Crystallized
In a splintered armchair.

The dark shades stand around me
Like unlighted skyscrapers,
Further and nearer than blocks away,
Saying I like that
As if they meant it.

Remote reflections in the rain.
But real shadows, like the summer,
The summer awash in trees,
And only a block away.

New York
Summer, 1967

On two tenterhooks,
He shores himself up on
Space, then leans on it,
A wall that gives.

In the stockstill air
Windows bid for
Fragments of sky
White as tickertape.

He leans far out up there
As if on a heeling yacht,
Belted behind a taut
Topsail of windowglass.

The airconditioners above
Drip spray between
His feet parted on nothing,
Spit in his eye.

He does battle
With the dusts of time,
And winces only
At the window-wiping birds.

WINDOWS IN MANHATTAN

I.

Abstracted,
These living daylights
Dwell within, yet
Independent of each other.
Cliffs of windows
Blacken the dark-blue sky.
All are recollections of
A same heaven's several climates:
Cloudy, lavender-black, or
Grey-glutted with snow.
Awash with stars, flushed
By the moon and all the planets,
Glass ground by dust and rain,
Glazed by more than glass,
Fluttered by flags
Of birds, papers, leaves,
Ribboned with movies,
Rivers, nebulae.

These fantasies persist
Because their roots are **gravity**,
The gravamen and ground
Of cities built on rock.

II.

Spires of compacted crystal, tilted
Backwards over pits, their own shadows,
Shadow each other:
Shadows of sunlit mountains cast
On shadowless flanks of sunlit mountains;
Shadows of continents of cloud
Covering entire, passing lakes
Of breeze-blown water skimmed
By flocks of angels.

They connect like
Mirrors confronted,
Reeling with electric news,
Revealing (vulnerable
Eyes wincing in
The sun of stony brows)
Passive or unwilling
Interest in one another, but still
An interest, like that of the casual
People-watchers, passers-by:
A detached correspondence
(Cool, correct, composed)
With others in the same situation,
All in the same unsinkable
Lifeboat of an island.

III.

These windows do not open.
They both see and look.
They wink at one another,
Communicate, across chasms
Sparkled with dust and dewdrops, that
Can hardly be said to yawn.
Their stacks of lighted metal,
Oblong icebergs about to slide,
Look forbidding and
Too blankly symmetrical
Until they are humanized
By a wild office-girl's
Half-pulled drapes,
By being broken
In the leaning avalanches of
Their semblances, abysses
Compounded and suspended
Like fates, judgements,
In the bare gaze of their brothers,
Hypocritical readers of themselves
Who weigh, reflect,
Accept, do not condemn.

IV.

As I move among them,
Unseen and unrecorded,
They distantly proceed,
Lofty and alone.
Like meteors or mountains,
Their interest is not involved.
They move within one another,
Move and have each other's being
In sheets of vertical water,
Fuming banks, niagaras of steam
In misty lochs and glens of air,
Fjords of effulgence
Eroded by the builders
Whose remote cornices conspire
Between one cloud and the next
T-squared scaffolds,
Cranes like gallows
To hang man by the neck
Over sheer stopgaps,
Girdered maildrops.

Demolition or construction?
As I move within them,
Caught in their roots' glassy mazes
As in a jungle of
Revolving drumdoors whirring,
Stirring and mingling like leafy
Falls of blood and sudden
Fountains of sap, I see in them
Trees lining summer estuaries
Through which a rambling water
Saunters like second sight,
Flows glitteringly, filtered and controlled
By dams of air, into
Dynamos and cataracts of light.

V.

I walk among them
As among the underwater shades
Of serpents and mammoths,
A drowned man stumbling
Ever deeper over his own shadow,
A shambling diver in suspended dance
Entangled in his cordages of bubbles
Who scans the rim of day, a slit
In the pondering of noon,
And scrapes the traffic of his sky
For a new breath, a fresh look.

To a drowning man,
These rooted flowers of glass
Seem to ripple on their stems,
Certainly to soar,
But downwards.

VI.

Stacked like displays
Of canned goods in
Massing cumuli,
The weather, deep-frozen,
Survives within their panes,
Geometric washing in a wind
That cannot shake them, cannot dry
The wet night of their powdered lakes.

Snow on sills, ready to drop,
Melting into steady downpours drip
Dripping on our hair-partings,
Our held-out hands, from
Toolrooms in airconditioned cliffs.
We hold our hands palm-down
In petrified pronation.
What ashen rains
May grind these visions into blindness?

Lined with gold,
The laundromatted clouds
Turn battlemented hems.
What immaterial
Matériel?

Even as we wake, lost shadows,
In darkness at the bottom of our
Wells of sleep and earth,

Sometimes the opposite
Topmost windows tell us,
Like Alps articulate
In Africa and Asia,
That there is light still in the world.

Blocks of rosy amber poised
On deeps of death
Launch us upwards into birth,
Into visionary orbits of
Another morning out of sight
But in our minds.

*

Park Avenue, Lexington,
Madison, Broadway,
Avenue of the Americas.

IN THE HOUSE OF EMILY DICKINSON

At this small table, hardly
Bigger than a checkerboard,
She told with birdlike hand
The coming of the word.

Over the square-paned casement
A muslin curtain, bright and still.
A hedge away, the country lane,
The fields, the railroad of the will.

She could see out, but they
Could not see in. The heart's long mile
Was all she trod, her world a room.
It did not cramp her style.

A spirit here was not confined,
But wandered high and far,
From yards of death to leagues of life,
From slowest candle to the quickest star.

ELEGY FOR EMILY

Robed in her usual white, withdrawn
In her white casket she was borne
Out of the sunny back door, over the lawn,
Along the ferny bridlepaths of May
To the burial ground on Pleasant Street.

The Irish workmen, her friends and servants,
Conducted her in a funeral like a game,
Some grave children's celebration,
The toecaps of their black boots
Burnished with buttercups.

O she was strange and rare
As a Red Indian brave—dark hair,
Pale face, great eyes, rich mouth.
At her throat, she wore in death
A posy of violets, and one pink cypripedium.

With two heliotropes by her hand
She floated over the pansied grass;
Through the hedge of flowering may
Fled like a flock of linnets,
Leaving behind her a buzz of bees.

The sun shone in her grave sprigged with yew,
Scented with earth and flowering trees.
Dark hair, pale face, great eyes, rich mouth.
—Her burial was an ascension, for
It is she now who remains, and we,
Alone, are the departed.

AT THE GRAVE OF EMILY DICKINSON

Leaving the florist's on the other side of Pleasant Street
With a posy of corn, thistles, rushes, pink immortelles,
I cross the vulgar road you would not recognize, and turn

Into the burial ground. Behind its black iron railings
Your father's tall stone still casts his shadow over you.
But on your other side, Lavinia—one you loved.

Being apart, in this hilly Amherst graveyard haunted
By weathered flags on worn tombs of forgotten warriors,
Flags whose faded stripes, extinguished stars

The sunset glows through as if they were of glass—
Surrounded by obelisks, yews, maples aflame with fall,
Congregationalist, you lie with them, and lie apart.

Below the yew, your father's stone, bolt upright. But yours
And Lavinia's lean back a little, half-fastidiously.
'Called back,' says the inscription. (Whither?) 'May 15, 1886.'

Upon your tomb I pressed two autumn leaves, gathered from my
      garden,
But the wind flung them away. Behind your tilted stone
I planted the posy of corn, thistles, rushes, pink immortelles.

I have come all this way across the world to speak to you,
As you so often came to speak to me, but found you
Not quite there: myself, remote and blind, not there at all.

Why am I telling you this? As the tears finally flow for you,
I know you are with me, as always, watching these words I write
To one who was also not altogether of this world.

LOS ANGELES

Preconditioned by assault and battery
In this bright cavern of the movies,
The talk of skytops and airborne expressways
Is the commerce of human souls
That in their separate compartments
Conduct the expected conversations.

At automotive moments, rape
And murder prick the concrete mask,
The rigid steel, the icy glass
With radiant spaces, smiles,
Shouts, words, laughter, screams—
Moments that are holes of sun.

Inhabitants of concrete deserts,
They take to the pistol and the knife
Like children sticking with pins
The black paper of a box of walls
Through which the light of sun and stars
Not only shines, but kills.

LEGENDS

CHRIST REJECTED

In the life of the ugly,
The plain, the lonely, sometimes
A stranger of great beauty comes
With an ease almost holy.

They who were never loved,
Who worshipped from afar with scorn
The beauty of the nobly-born
For a moment felt themselves moved.

How can it be? Who is he?
A stranger of great beauty,
With limbs perfect, smile all purity,
Comes, and gives his love to me?

It is as they tell us of
Jesus, loving the halt and the dumb,
Who, laying his hands upon lepers, did come
On earth, to give us of God's love.

How beautiful are thy feet with shoes.
The joints of thy thighs are as jewels,
The smell of thy nose like apples.
His legs are pillars of marble, his lips lilies . . .

The ugly believe, and know
That this is the love of Christ.
—But put an arm about the stranger's waist,
He melts away like snow.

The stranger of great beauty comes
And goes in lives that are plain,
Bringing love, but also fear; hope, but pain.
Ours are the hearts, but his the drums.

None can resist him, who are not
As perfect as he, but those sad fools
Who turn away as he comes with smiles,
And seek the comfort of the brothers he forgot.

THE BEAUTIFUL STRANGERS

(after sighting an Unidentified Flying Object)

They are above us,
Beyond us and around us,
Out of space out of time.

Between star and star,
New moons, and beings wiser
Than ourselves, approach.

Our earth is rotten
As a fruit about to drop
Into nothingness.

They are gardeners
Of space, who come to tend us.
Strangers, they love us.

In ages long past
They came to our planet.
We drove them away.

Ever since that day
Our world moves to destruction.
Death grows among us.

Only if we call
To the beautiful strangers
Will our peace return.

I know they watch me
As I write this poem now.
Poets are cosmic.

I feel their silence
Like words, their absence like love.
I belong not to this earth.

I belong to them, and they
Are my brothers, their space my home
That is not of this earth.

Ever a stranger, I came
From further fields, an outer place
Whose clouds I trail to death.

Ever a white shadow wandering
On this lost world, white and alone
Among the crowding shades of black,

My one voice cries to you, men
Of earth, out of my solitude,
That we must turn to them.

We must watch for them.
We must give our hearts and souls,
Open eyes and arms.

Look to the heavens
And upon the ground for signs.
They are among us as I am among you.

And we shall see them
With the eyes of vision, if
We have sense to see.

And we shall know them
By their purity and grace,
If we have hearts to feel.

Where are my lost brothers?
Let them come back to me!
Let us return to them!

They are above us,
Beyond us and around us,
Out of space out of time.

SPACE CHILD SIGHTING REPORTED DURING HEAVY BLIZZARD

Skidding down
On power lines,
Hovering in
His little craft,
Beaming in on us,
Then at the velocity
Of fright, flashing
Out of sight.

This was the boy
(Or girl) who came
This winter eve, on
Saturday night at the
Local, leaving nothing
But a blackened patch
At this touchdown in
The shepherds' field
Of snowy sheep, and
A couple of stunned
Beasts, an ox and an ass.
—This came to pass.

THE SEASONS OF CHRISTMAS

Love in the springtime
Fired from afar
The boy from a new
Discovered star.

Summer long
With the grass he grew.
When the grass was mown
With the wind he flew.

Autumn long
When the pear trees groan,
He hung and hallowed,
His mother's son.

An angel from space
With the winter came.
The world was dumb.
He was born in shame.

THE RIDDLES OF CHRISTMAS

How can a boy
Be king, yet lie in a manger?

How can a child be loved,
Yet die as a stranger?

How can he hansel the gifts
Of kings, and yet be poor?

How can his life
Be brief, and yet endure?

How can there hang a star
Where none blazed in the sky?

How can a man
Be born, yet never die?

Who is this stranger comes
As if he knew us all our days?

Who is this child of man
Clothed in the light of space?

Answer is there none
But Christ, the All, the One?

THE NEW BABY

A Nativity for Now

Away in brown paper
A monster is born:
His bones black with strontium
His bowels all torn.

A test in the unclean sky
Showered dust where he lay
No nuclear deterrent
Keeps leukaemia at bay.

His heart is inhuman
His sex is obscure
The ox and the ass
Are six-headed for sure.

63

The little boy Jesus
No crying he makes
But the ox and the ass
Frighten him when he wakes.

His bald head inflated
With fallout so free
He's as radioactive
As an H-babe can be.

His mother's womb withered
And she burst with his birth,
Who was born blind to save us
From this hell here on earth.

RESURRECTION

It was only the gardener.
His hands were all caked with clay,
Dirt under the long nails,
His hair a sight,
All matted, looked as if
He hadn't had a wash
For days.

Clothes all soiled
And torn. No shoes.
You know the kind:
The typical dropout.
Dead beat.

He'd been sweating,
And the drops had streaked
The dust on his cheeks,
Drenched his beard.

(I do think they
Might wash more often.)

He'd scratched his forehead
On some thorns—probably
Pruning that thicket hedge
Beyond the wilderness.

(Well, that's his problem.
Nothing to do with us.
Anyhow, it was only the gardener.)

He was so filthy, he
Stank like a ditch.
His sleeves rolled up,
His muscles shivering, as if
He'd just been heaving
A ton of bricks.

(I must say, he was well built.
He had a good body on him.
If only they'd keep their hair clean!)

There was blood on his hands and feet.
Frankly, he was a mess.

At least he had a job.
He was the gardener.
They always have one
In that kind of place,
You know, to keep the graves tidy,
Keep an eye on things.

He had a flower in his hand,
A lily—or was it a daffodil?
For a minute I did wonder
If he'd been robbing a grave.

Never said a word.
Just looked right through us,
Proper standoffish.

(They have a nerve,
Honestly, these people.)

Mind you, it did cross my mind
He might have been in some
Sort of accident, like
Getting mugged, or
Busted by the cops.
Blood everywhere on him,
But, all dried up, so
I thought why worry.
None of my business.

Later, talking it over at
The new minister's after-service
Easter morning *kaffeeklatsch*, we
Decided he must have been barmy.
(They get like that, you know.
Don't know where you are
With people, these days,
Do you? Talk about weird!)

We had a good laugh.
These days, really,
You don't know who
You might meet, or
Who you're talking to.
You can't be bothering yourself
About every nut case you come across
Or you'd never have a minute's
Peace, would you?

And anyway,
It was only the gardener.

CONTRADICTIONS

HEINE IN RAMSGATE

Wandering the pre-Victorian sand,
He found the Channel tame and sly
After Cuxhaven, Helgoland,
The North Sea and Norderney.

'My heart is like the ocean . . .'
But not indifferent enough
To stomach Britain's bitter potion.
No *Reisebilder* came of London smut.

'Send a philosopher to London, he'll survive,'
Was his conclusion. 'Never
Send a poet: he's too much alive,
Too singular, too clever.'

England he could bear
Only a little while. Even
Germany the bad was better. Aware
Of his own apartness, heaven

For him was Paris—such a place
As Hamburg, Frankfurt, Düsseldorf or Munich
Had no inkling of. But *London*—his face,
Bony and bright and runic,

Glittered a moment on Golders Green
And was gone, towards the exile's final fear on earth:
That dreams or death will cause his spirit to be seen
Haunting the hated fatherland that gave him birth.

VLADIMIR ASHKENAZY

Solo, with hanging arms he
Strides to the lacquered instrument's
Longdistance locomotive platform.

Engine blackly throbs and
Tingles as it waits, posed for
Flight, on slight gilt pedals.

*

Already in blunt fingertips
He spells the future's progressions,
Dwells on yielding rubato

In the entirely legato
Andante spianato. Sits:
Feels in forearms the tracks

Of muscled fingerings,
Athletic grip plundering bright
Fistfuls of keys. Plays:

Telling in wrists
Most tactful of all
In all their sinewy hinges

The tones, allegro vivace
Or tenderly moderato
Of man's first performance.

The heart's caprice,
Tenses of breathing,
Attack of a kiss, mute

Hesitations, accords
Of desire and dream,
Inventions, fantasies and fugues

70

Recapitulations of
The recapitulated, the
Compulsive coda, motif

Of themes developed far
Past statement, the night's white
Cataracts, cadenzas, plunging us

Back to where we started—
In the bones before
Birth, before conception.

*

After the Schubert sonata
The Études without fault
The Prokofiev hullabaloo

Stands, bull-shouldered, and
To a rolling tempo, solo,
Biting a broken nail

Strides from the lacquered lake
That throbs and tingles, echoing still
To the clutch of his long haul.

*

Returns reluctantly to
Stroke the scented fur
Of one posthumous mazurka.

Tokyo
November, 1967

THE SUNKEN PIANOFORTE

Dust drifting piano keys
Depressed in dunes of sand.
The lifted lid of the grand
A desolate bay
Tilted on vacancies,
The crater of a day.

Fingers dredge those chords
Like silted steps, black and white,
Whose treads, bared by the sea's height,
Sink and drown beneath the shells
Of sound, release no words
In stillness's recurrent bells.

Speech cannot hear
And hearing cannot tell
The whole of hell.
Only the tramping hands
On shores of dust and clay
Can touch it, veiled in sands.

A WINTER FOOL

With countenance pallid and stiff
As white horses in dawns of rime
Or public clock on townhall cliff
He steps as on stilts in snows of time.

A football of frozen stones
Splits the world before his eyes.
The blood that tints his bones
To chill gems on his forehead dries.

The castle walls are velvet black,
The sky is flocked with leaden cloud.
He leaves a dark and lonely track
That trails his shadow in the crowd.

He steps like an orphan in the park,
His faded clothes are torn and thin
As last leaves, dead and dark,
That patch a scarecrow harlequin.

MOONFLIGHT

You three kings
Of orient are?

You bring no gifts
Of scent and spice. Only
Machines, the Star
Spangled Banner, science,
The common cold.

The star you follow
Has no wonder at its root,
No mystery ablaze
With warmth and light.

Only a dim desert,
Reflection of our present
Earthlight gloom.

A true star
Cannot be touched.

Nor are you anything like
Puck or Ariel, as you plod
In those unsmart coveralls
Wired for sweat, excrement,
Dehydrated drinks,
Airconditioned oxygen.

Your ponderous capsule
Could no more vanish into
Air, into thin air, than
A load of coal.

Radio wisecracks,
College boy humour
Are preferable to your sinister
Readings from the scriptures.
Take the Bible to the moon?

Moon missionaries.

And we know what follows missionaries
In the colonies of space:
Trade. Commerce. Politics.
Exploitation of the natives.
Degeneration of local arts and crafts.
A loss of legends.
The noisy misery of war.
Conquest.
Independence.
Emergent starvation.
Death.

'Some Wiltshire rustics,
Seeing the figure of the moon
In a pond, attempted to
Rake it out . . .'

Better, like the oriental
Mystic, to point
A finger at the moon, and
Do nothing but laugh.

So keep your noses out of
What is none of your business, will you?
Leave the moon to poets and astrologers,
And to those Three Wise Men
Who came, remember,
Not from the West, but
From the rising sun.

Stay home, you hometown boys!
The East is rising,
And it is the sun.